And You Can Love Me

A STORY FOR EVERYONE WHO LOVES SOMEONE WITH ASD

SHERRY QUAN LEE

ILLUSTRATED BY
TEAGAN "TRIF" MERRIFIELD

LETTERING BY
KYRA GAYLOR

Library of Congress Cataloging-in-Publication Data

Names: Lee, Sherry Quan, 1948- author. | Merrifield, Teagan (Trif),
    illustrator.
Title: And you can love me : a story for everyone who loves someone with
    autism spectrum disorder (ASD) : a picture book / by Sherry Lee ;
    illustrated by Teagan ("Trif") Merrifield.
Description: Ann Arbor, MI : Loving Healing Press, [2019] | Summary: An
    autistic boy celebrates "another year of being me."
Identifiers: LCCN 2018054649 (print) | LCCN 2018058687 (ebook) | ISBN
    9781615994267 (Kindle, ePub, pdf) | ISBN 9781615994250 | ISBN
    9781615994250(hardcover :alk. paper) | ISBN 9781615994243(paperback
    :alk. paper) | ISBN 9781615994267(eBook)
Subjects: | CYAC: Autism--Fiction.
Classification: LCC PZ7.1.L428 (ebook) | LCC PZ7.1.L428 An 2019 (print) | DDC
    [E]--dc23
LC record available at https://lccn.loc.gov/2018054649

Published by
Loving Healing Press   www.LHPress.com
5145 Pontiac Trail   info@LHPress.com
Ann Arbor, MI 48105

Tollfree (USA/CAN): 888-761-6268
Fax: 734-663-4173

Distributed by: Ingram Book Group (USA/CAN/AU), Bertram's Books (UK/EU)

Dedication

to my nonverbal autistic grandson and his parents

to everyone who loves someone with ASD

"If you've met one person with autism, you've met one person with autism."

— Dr. Stephen Shore,
Assistant Professor at Adelphi University, Garden City, NY

I am
Ethan.

Today I am another year of being me.

The me that
I am
is silent.

And you can love me.

The me that I am welcomes the beat of my hands clapping.

the table,

the chair,

and the bounce

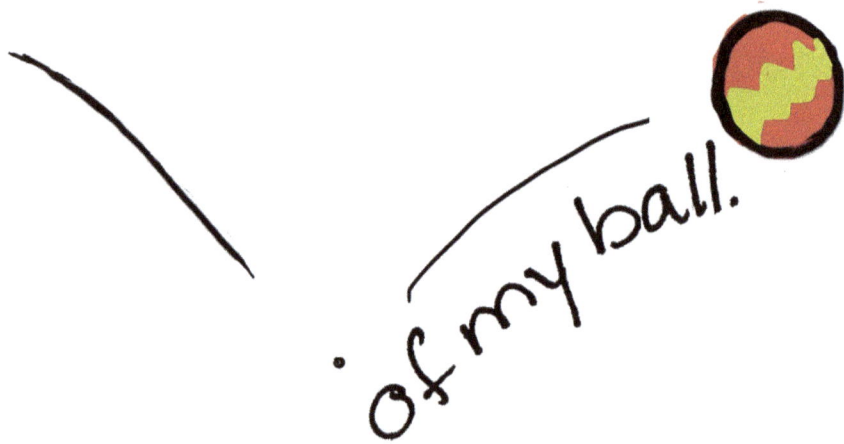

of my ball.

Enter my world
and get to know me.

Enter my world
and you can hold me.

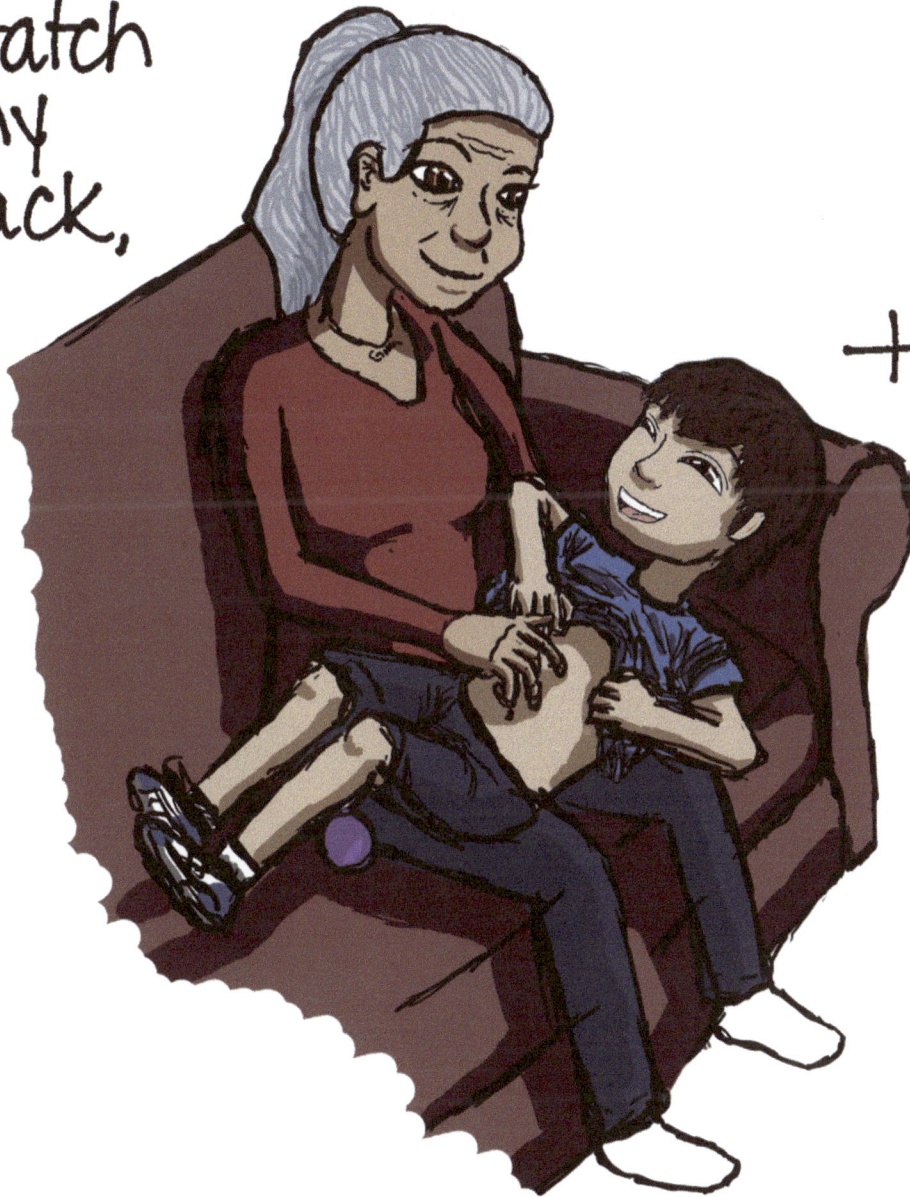

Hold my hand and I will lead you. I will show you I am hungry.

I will show
  you I want to be free.

What helps the me
that I am from
morning to moon?

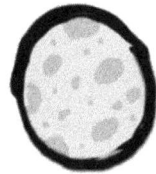
Bouncing a ball.

Balls are hiding everywhere.

Any ball
any color
any size.

Hand to ball.
Clap!

Ball to hand.
Clap!

I am
Ethan.

You can see in my eyes
and know in your heart

that I'm in the world of Ethan.

And you can love me.

About Autism

"Autism, or autism spectrum disorder (ASD), refers to a broad range of conditions characterized by challenges with social skills, repetitive behaviors, speech and nonverbal communication."

www.AutismSpeaks.org/what-autism

"Autism Spectrum Disorder (ASD) is a developmental disorder that causes issues with communication, social, verbal, and motor skills. The most important thing to know about autism is that it is a spectrum disorder, meaning its effects vary from person to person. No two people with autism have the same symptoms. Symptoms generally appear in the early stage of childhood before the age of three."

www.MyAutism.org/all-about-autism/what-is-autism/

"Autism spectrum disorder (ASD) is a complex developmental condition that involves persistent challenges in social interaction, speech and nonverbal communication, and restricted/repetitive behaviors. The effects of ASD and the severity of symptoms are different in each person."
www.psychiatry.org/patients-families/autism/what-is-autism-spectrum-disorder

Contributors

Sherry Quan Lee, MFA, University of Minnesota, is the author of *Chinese Blackbird, a memoir in verse*, *Love Imagined: a mixed race memoir* (a Minnesota Book Award Finalist); and, editor of *How Dare We! Write: a multicultural creative writing discourse*.

Teagan "Trif" Merrifield attended Minneapolis Media Arts Institute for computer modeling. Her passion is bringing what's inside of the mind to life. *And You Can Love Me* is her first venture into picture book illustration.

Kyra Gaylor studied education at Southwest Minnesota State University. Most of her teaching experience has been at the kindergarten and preschool levels. She loves to create. She loves to collect and repurpose vintage treasures.

www.ingramcontent.com/pod-product-compliance
Lightning Source LLC
Chambersburg PA
CBHW041426270326
41931CB00023B/3495